I recommend ... world, for it w... and enrich their lives. It is the scholarly writing of a scientist, diplomat, and artist directed primarily at the youth. The success which Dr. Edmunds holds up for the youth is one that has them expanding their horizons beyond their immediate environment to that of the wider world and has them delving into the vast area of knowledge with the consequent enrichment of their lives. I hope several young people will find pleasure and inspiration in the words of Dr. Edmunds. I also hope that although the publication is directed primarily at the young, the older persons who are still young at heart will find pleasure in reading it as well.

Sir George Alleyne
Chancellor of the University of the West Indies

Dr. Edmunds' Triangle of Success could be aptly entitled "Everyone's Guide to Self-Fulfillment." It touches on three guiding principles which all of us need to embrace as we proceed in one's life journey. I associate myself with the guiding principles of the book, principles which I have shared with my students over the years. The formula of success embodied in this book takes us to the very limit of ourselves, and then beyond ourselves to join with the rest of the humanity in that continuous exercise of enriching our lives and improving our circumstances. The humbling realization that knowledge is infinite and our ignorance perhaps no less, is motivating enough to make all of us life-long learners.

Dame Pearlette Louisy
Governor General
St. Lucia

The educational philosophical thrust of *The Triangle of Success* reflects the shared commitment of Medgar Evers College of the City university of New York, to ensure the emergence of this generation's adolescent community into future leaders and entrepreneurs of our city. Your book presents sound moral and ethical values needed to empower our youth to accomplish success. It is a welcoming contribution to the children of African descent, especially in urban settings.

Edison Jackson
President
Medgar Evers College
of the City University of New York

Against the backdrop of negative peer influence and counter-productive distractions of technology and media, J. Edsel Edmunds has offered here a paradigm of success for our young generation in schools and university campuses worldwide.

j.a. Irish
Professor
Director of the Caribbean Research Center
Medgar Evers College
Of the City University of New York

Eloquent and original. Inspiring and empowering. A blueprint for success for use in High Schools and Colleges.

N. G. Duncan
Professor
College of New Rochelle
New York

> **--FOR OUR YOUTH --**
>
> **--LEADERS OF TOMORROW --**

THE TRIANGLE
OF
SUCCESS

J. EDSEL EDMUNDS, Ph.D.

> A Paradigm of Success for
> Our Young Generation
> Dr. George Irish

This book is a work of non-fiction. Unless otherwise noted, the author and the publisher make no explicit guarantees as to the accuracy of the information contained in this book and in some cases, names of people and places have been altered to protect their privacy.

© *2006 J. Edsel Edmunds. All Rights Reserved.*

No part of this book may be reproduced, stored in a retrieval system, or transmitted by any means without the written permission of the author.

First published by AuthorHouse 08/22/06

ISBN: 1-4208-7549-3 (sc)

Printed in the United States of America
Bloomington, Indiana

This book is printed on acid-free paper.

1663 LIBERTY DRIVE, SUITE 200
BLOOMINGTON, INDIANA 47403
(800) 839-8640
WWW.AUTHORHOUSE.COM

ACKNOWLEDGMENTS

The author expresses appreciation to Mrs. Lucy Mohamed-Edmunds, Adjunct Professor at the University of the District of Columbia, in Washington, DC for inviting him to address her students of English as a Second Language (ESL) as an exercise in listening, speaking, and writing, as well as, a motivation and empowerment exercise. He thanks her for urging him to publish his lectures and for the initial editing of the same.

The editorial and content inputs of the following persons are appreciated:

Maria Jenkins (Principal Editor), Leo Edwards, Francis Leonce, Lydia Anslm, Gregor Williams, Lewis Campbell, Alison Moses and Ernest Mabrey.

DEDICATION

This booklet is dedicated to junior and senior high school students, university students and youth groups in their aspiration to achieve success in the face of many challenges.

It is also dedicated to students of English as a Second Language (ESL) who inspired its publication, and to the less privileged students of our world.

INTRODUCTION

This publication is a summary of lectures given by the author to students at junior and senior high schools, colleges and universities. It came about at the invitation of Mrs. Lucy Mohamed-Edmunds, Adjunct Professor at The University of the District of Columbia (UDC) and Montgomery County Public Schools (MCPS), to lecture to her English as a Second Language (ESL) classes in Speaking, Listening, Reading, and Writing.

The substance of the lectures was designed to inspire and motivate students, while at the same time giving them an opportunity to interact with the lecturer in their speaking and listening classes. These lectures were used in assessing their comprehension and ability to write on the subjects covered.

In the course of his lectures, the author made reference to his educational background from high school in his island home, St. Lucia, in the Caribbean, to his academic training, and to his achievements at Universities in the

United States. The scope and relevance of his areas of study were explained and his work experiences in the international arena were outlined. He ended his lectures by urging students to develop meaningful hobbies and made reference to his hobbies - poetry and painting - by reading some of his poems and showing some of his works of art.

The Triangle of Success is meant to motivate and inspire students and youth, in general, to achieve success through the use of basic principles emanating from the author's knowledge and experience.

TABLE OF CONTENTS

OUR COMMON BEING 1

UNDERSTANDING DIFFERENCES 7

THE ROAD TO SUCCESS 13

GOAL SETTING 19

BELIEF-IN-SELF 25

ACTION PLAN 29

PERSONAL ATTRIBUTES AND
OUTREACH BEYOND SELF 35

FOLLOWERS/LEADERS 45

THE DIAMETER OF KNOWLEDGE:
THE AREA OF THE UNKNOWN 51

DEVELOP A HOBBY 57

SELECTED RELATED PRESENTATIONS
BY AUTHOR 63

OUR COMMON BEING

> WE ARE ALL OF A COMMON BEING AT BIRTH, RESULTING FROM DIFFERENT COMBINATIONS OF SPERM AND EGG; THE TIME, PLACE, AND CIRCUMSTANCE ARE NOT OF OUR DOING.

OUR COMMON BEING

Since this publication is directed at persons from different countries, ethnic backgrounds, religions, social and economic circumstances, I find it necessary to draw attention to a fundamental fact of our being. In order to highlight this fact, I would like you to pause a while and think about the many different faces one encounters on a daily basis.

The fundamental fact is that we all look different. I refer here to our external appearance – that which we can observe. As an exercise, you may even wish to describe the details of our different external appearances. This is but a superficial analysis of what we all are and does not tell us anything about our inner qualities, nor our humanness i.e. what we are as human beings.

The fact is that we all have one thing in common - we belong to the human race – we are all classified in the animal kingdom as *Homo sapiens* regardless of our place of origin, ethnicity, religion, culture, or place in society. This is a fundamental fact which we must all remember. We all belong to the same animal specie.

We came about as a result of the union of a sperm with an egg, resulting in (after several changes at the microscopic level) our development through embryonic stages and the phenomenon of birth - the commonality of our beginning.

What I wish to impress upon you is that we were all born of the union of a sperm and an egg. More importantly, is the fact that none of us is responsible for our birth. We had no part to play in our origins. Think again about our daily encounters with human beings in order to absorb the reality of our different appearances; at the same time, contemplate on the commonality of our humanness, though born at different times, in different places, and under different circumstances.

Unfortunately, there are still some people who blame their birth for their present position in life when they had no control over it. We were not responsible for our birth in time and place. We must accept our being here and constantly seek to improve our present and

The Triangle of Success

future positions in the world in which we now find ourselves.

Following from the above, we must not feel inferior to anyone. Some are born into wealth, others into poverty, and others somewhere in between. There are enough good examples of success stories regarding persons born under different circumstances to spur us to achieve great things in life, regardless of our origins. There are those who were born of humble beginnings and have become great leaders and contribute enormously to society. There are also those who have overcome great adversity and disabilities and have mastered various fields with excellence. We have living examples of those successes in this world which should give us strength to overcome any deficiencies we may have. We must therefore not feel inferior to anyone.

There is nothing wrong in reflecting on our past with a view to bettering ourselves and our fellow beings for the future. Unfortunately, there are too many who continuously mope over the past and their origins with negative thoughts about themselves. There are also some who justify their actions against other human beings based upon their birthplace, religion, ethnicity, and past history. This attitude has had and is having sad implications on national, regional, and global conflicts. It results in loss of lives, suffering, and the break down of peaceful relations among peoples, regions, and nations.

The above realizations are important for the application of the triangle of success.

UNDERSTANDING DIFFERENCES

> **THROUGH AN UNDERSTANDING OF THE ENORMOUS DIVERSITY OF HUMANKIND, WE CAN CONTRIBUTE TO A REDUCTION IN HUMAN CONFLICTS AND TO WORLD PEACE**

UNDERSTANDING DIFFERENCES

As we grow up in a particular environment, we naturally become influenced by its dimensions. The influence may be parental or societal. We have all been influenced in some way by our religious upbringing, the language spoken at home or in our neighborhood, the culture, and other human manifestations of our environment.

In our early life, we therefore developed different eating habits, different clothing preferences, and even different ways of walking and expressing ourselves. All these traits were either imposed upon us or subconsciously acquired in our formative years. They were strong external or environmental influences, to the extent that they may have become so deeply ingrained in us to cause resistance to change.

Some of us, depending upon how long we remained under the influence of our early environment, have never changed those acquired traits. Some of us have become so overpowered by those influences that the thought of change is never entertained. On the other hand, some of us, as a result of various new influences and exposure to different horizons, have been able to modify our behavior and attitudes through various human experiences and have adapted to different situations and circumstances.

In the course of my studies, I became acquainted with a friend who through his religious upbringing was a strict vegetarian. One day, after three years of knowing and observing his strict adherence to his religious beliefs, my wife and I saw him at a McDonalds restaurant eating a substantial hamburger. We were surprised and so was he to be seen by us eating meat. We, therefore, asked him to explain such a change from his deep religious belief. He looked at us with a smile and made the profound statement that it took him three years to realize that the American cow was not sacred. We recommended to him that, following the trend of his statement, his country should start a trade with America by importing American cows and exporting cows from his country to the United States, since Americans would have no regard for the sacred values of his cows. His reply was that very few from his country would conform to his way of thinking.

As we travel to different countries or observe others on television, it becomes evident that human differences exist and we sometimes take them for granted. Most times we think of ourselves as the norm and the others as deviants. I recall observing a student writing his sentences in a different direction compared to the way I was taught. I commented to him that his writing method was rather odd. He laughingly informed me that my form of writing looked rather odd to him and is far removed from earlier writings of the civilized world. In effect he educated me to the fact that my norm was not his norm or the norm of millions of his people. He opened my mind to the need to understand other people and their cultures.

It is therefore important that, while we must understand the commonality of the fact of our birth, we must also understand the enormous diversity of humankind which surrounds us. I contend that some of the conflicts facing the world today at the national, regional, and international levels, result from a lack of information or understanding of the differences among people, nations, and regions. It is my view that our world leaders should pay closer attention to the understanding of the different cultures and circumstances of the different people and countries which make up our world of today.

In so doing, we may be able to reduce world conflict and "man's inhumanity to man". Through an understanding of the human factors related to human development, and the influences of ethnic, cultural, and socio-economic environments, we could develop a better appreciation of our differences and work towards amicable solutions to human problems.

Understanding differences is important for the achievement of success, for although we all belong to the same human race, we are different in many respects and are the result of a wide range of influences.

THE ROAD TO SUCCESS

THE ROAD TO SUCCESS*

In order to succeed in our world, regardless of place of birth and environmental influences, one must formulate some basic concepts and strategies.

One must develop a positive approach to life: belief in oneself, identify and take advantage of opportunities which present themselves, formulate well-defined goals, and work towards a plan of action to achieve those goals. I present this in what I call *The Triangle of Success,* illustrated in Figure 1.

It must be pointed out that the points of the triangle are not fixed and the starting point in the triangle may vary, depending upon the person or their prevailing circumstances. For example, as will be elucidated later, you may have to change your original goal depending on changing circumstances. This would lead to

---

*For purposes of this publication in the context of its application to our youth, to whom it is primarily addressed, success is interpreted as the favorable achievement of one's potential.

FIG 1

THE TRIANGLE OF SUCCESS

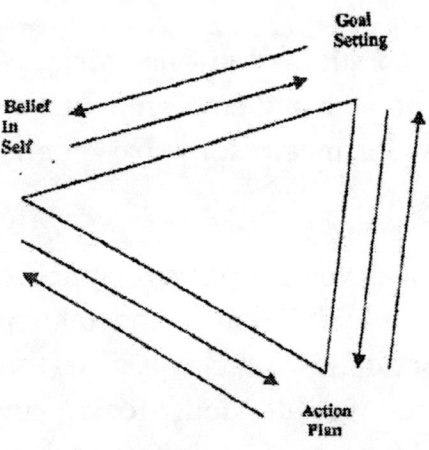

changes in your belief patterns, as they relate to newly set goals, as well as the necessary action plans which may follow. Therefore, each point of the triangle may have different directional flows depending upon different situations and differences in personalities.

It is recognized that success has different meanings to different persons. Nevertheless, bearing in mind that this book is dedicated to our youth in their formative years, I have decided to follow a sequence from goal setting to belief-in-self and the formulation of an action

The Triangle of Success

plan to achieve set goals, where the various points of the triangle are interdependent.

It may be argued that belief-in-self and presentation of opportunities may be prevailing factors in the start-up which leads to success. However, this does not remove nor diminish the inter-relatedness of the points of the triangle.

The concept of the triangle has its application in all human endeavors, at the personal, national, and international levels.

GOAL SETTING

> GOAL SETTING IS FUNDAMENTAL TO SUCCESS. IT MUST BE REALISTIC AND SUBJECT TO CHANGE IF CIRCUMSTANCES DICTATE. THERE ARE INNUMERABLE AVAILABLE OPPORTUNITIES

GOAL SETTING

It is important to set goals in life, but they must be realistic in intent and within your capabilities. For example, to become an engineer, you must acquire knowledge in mathematics and to be a doctor, you must acquire knowledge in biology. But though one may not have the ability or inclination to learn these subjects, there are several other fields which can be pursued. In addition, the initial goal may be hampered through lack of finance or various situations beyond one's control.

Therefore, there may be the need to deviate from your original goal and set new or related ones, which are more realistic, and in keeping with the circumstances. This does not constitute failure, but rather it is an indication of a realistic assessment of your capabilities in point of time. In synthesis, depending upon one's stage in life, different goals may be set, one leading to another, with a well-defined purpose.

J. Edsel Edmunds

When I completed high school, I contemplated studying to be either a medical doctor or a lawyer. I entertained the thought of pursuing these professions because I had the necessary subjects to enter a University for such studies. Nevertheless, I had to face the hard reality that my parents could not afford to finance my studies and also that the few fully financed scholarships in the country were already taken by other students.

One day, I read an advertisement about scholarships being offered to study Vocational Education in Agriculture at the University of Puerto Rico. I immediately changed my original goal and set my sights on the study of Agriculture rather than remaining static with a high school diploma. This was a difficult decision, for I realized that the language spoken in Puerto Rico was Spanish, which was not my mother tongue.

I accepted the scholarship to the University of Puerto Rico knowing full well that I would have to study a new language. The new professional goal, including the challenge of studying another language, was directly related to my personal circumstances and at that time, I never visualized what was to follow. Nevertheless, I applied *The Triangle of Success* at every stage in my various pursuits outlined in the section "About the Author".

I know of several successful persons in many fields, who at different stages in their lives, have changed their original goal for various reasons. Some have changed many times along the way while they sought to find themselves and their calling, or to give true expression to their aptitudes. In life, there are many avenues opened to us and we must sometimes make new decisions when necessary and seize the moment when it presents itself.

I also know of many professionals who, although successful in their academic pursuits, are very poor practitioners in their fields and a disgrace to their professions. There are others, who after graduating in a particular field, find greater joy in practicing other professions, and sometimes this is to the benefit of humanity. Yet, there are others, who in their burning desire to study a particular profession, never get over the hard facts of their not being able to accomplish their desires and have become psychologically imbalanced for life.

J. Edsel Edmunds

In all of this, we must remember that we cannot all be holders of university degrees. Our world would be very deficient and indeed non-functional without persons well trained in the vocational and technical fields. No matter how many academic degrees we may acquire, we need technical personnel to make our work operational.

BELIEF-IN-SELF

> POSITIVE THINKING, SELF-CONFIDENCE, SELF-ESTEEM, AND INNER DETERMINATION ARE HALLMARKS OF SUCCESS

BELIEF-IN-SELF

If you do not believe in yourself and do not have the self-determination to achieve your goals, you will not succeed. Inner determination and self-esteem are hallmarks of success. This requires the application of positive thinking as opposed to negative thinking which is self-destructive. The moment you develop doubts about yourself and about your ability to succeed, when in fact you have what it takes, you are starting on the downward slope to failure. Self-confidence and positive thinking are necessary for self-fulfillment.

Every step we take along the road of life must be accompanied by an inner feeling of self-confidence. Each goal that we set must have that winning element of belief that we can make it. This may call for adjustment to new, different, and, sometimes very challenging circumstances. If you fail in one field, you should try another, for there are many streams of opportunities awaiting your discovery. Change direction, set new goals, test the waters, and keep moving on.

I know of many successful persons today, who flunked out of school, tried a new direction, and eventually found their true calling. There are some who made millions of dollars in their newly found ventures after initial failures. Today, they are contributing to humanity in many different ways. If they did not have confidence in themselves they would have remained as failures in the society and perhaps causing more harm than good.

Self-determination, self-confidence, self-esteem, and inner drive are all important for success. We should, therefore, not be discouraged by failure or intimidated by the lofty achievements of others. We each have different propensities and capabilities. The greatness is within us to succeed no matter our line of human endeavor or stage in life.

ACTION PLAN

> **THERE IS NO SUBSTITUTE FOR HARD WORK. THERE MUST BE AN ACTION PLAN DIRECTED AT THE ACHIEVEMENT OF GOALS**

ACTION PLAN

This area refers to the steps you need to take in the achievement of your goals. When I was young, I was told that placing books under my pillow at nights would not result in the absorption of their contents. I learnt that there is no substitute for reading, listening, absorbing new knowledge, and understanding what you read, hear, and observe, at the same time recognizing that there is so much we do not know.

Your action plan must be accompanied by a disciplined mind which is focused on your goal. You will have to overcome the obstacles to your progress and the many distractions which will present themselves. You will have to find a balance between work and play, not letting either one lead to an imbalance in your life. Remain focused and walk that extra mile, which is not as long as you may think when you consider the lasting rewards that could be achieved at the end of the road.

J. Edsel Edmunds

An action plan takes you from point A to point B and to other points along the way. You may have to re-examine your plan from time to time. I remember when I first went to New York and was told to take the A train to get to my destination. I got caught up in the flow of humanity in the underground station and in my anxiety took the AA train thinking that the other A was for emphasis. As the train moved along I did not see the various landmarks which I was expected to see, so I got off the train and sought new directions. My action plan was flawed and I had to retrace my steps.

We must be clear in our plan of action and not drift in the current of a river without knowing where we are going. We must not allow ourselves to be randomly carried away in uncharted directions. Our plan must be well formulated, but when we discover that we are going adrift we must pause to reconsider our actions and plans and oft times take new directions.

This takes me to the area of listening. I must admit that I did not listen carefully to the directions given to me on my trip to New York. You may be surprised to learn that few

The Triangle of Success

people actually listen and digest what is being said. They often say "I hear you" but they have not listened and digested what is being said.

This is probably why it is often necessary to repeat certain things over and over before an idea or the substance being conveyed sinks into our system. Sometimes our own thoughts dominate our thinking and our opinions do not easily give way to the thoughts of others when they speak to us. There is much we can learn by listening to others, but we must be able to distinguish the good from the bad.

In all of the above, we should open ourselves to sound advice and inject realism into our action plan.

PERSONAL ATTRIBUTES AND OUTREACH BEYOND SELF

THE WORLD NEEDS THAT HUMAN EMBRACE OF UNDERSTANDING, LOVE, AND PEACE.
REACH OUT TO HELP OTHERS BEYOND SELF

PERSONAL ATTRIBUTES AND OUTREACH BEYOND SELF

The Triangle of Success will not be operative unless you develop some positive attitudes about yourselves and those with whom you interact. Too often some people suffer from self-pity. If you pause to think of the human suffering the world over, the millions of starving children, some doomed to die at an early age, you will realize how fortunate you are to be alive, and to have achieved your level of education with the possibilities of a bright future ahead. It is estimated that hundreds of thousands of children die every day through malnutrition and starvation and millions die yearly through wars of one kind or another and civil strife.

I, therefore, wish to impress upon you, that you should take advantage of every opportunity available to improve yourself and try to excel in what you do. If you do not succeed in a particular area of human endeavor, take it as a challenge, marshal your resources, and follow a different course of action.

You have available to you many opportunities to better yourself. Set your goals, change them when circumstances dictate, believe in yourself, and, above all, formulate an action plan directed towards your goals.

Perhaps your focus is on making money and you measure our success by the color of the dollar. I would like to impress upon you that the color of success is gray, not green, for our measure of success will depend upon how you use the gray matter of your brain towards the achievements of your goals.

This takes us back to *The Triangle of Success* within the context of the use of our brainpower to set realistic goals, with a strong self-belief, awareness of our capabilities and the organization of action plans to achieve our goals.

Self-discipline, self-confidence, and self-esteem have been alluded to in previous sections. These attributes by themselves will not make a better world for ourselves or for humanity as a whole, for we do not live in isolation. We live with others within a human family, and therefore we must relate to others and respect their humanness. We must show concern for others with a sense of forgiveness, understanding, and giving. Unfortunately, our world is becoming more and more self-centered at the individual, national, and international levels. Self-interest is so rampant at those levels that the gap between the haves and the have-nots is widening and human suffering is increasing. As a result, there is increasing discontent and social unrest all over the world.

In our present world of "globalization" – a word which is so often misused by some of our world leaders – our relationship with others should assume a global dimension. This requires an outreach of the human spirit beyond our immediate environment, communities, and nations in a wide embrace of humankind.

The world needs that human embrace of understanding, love, and peace across borders and superimposed boundaries. Global humanism in our private lives, in public policy, and international affairs, can go a long way in reducing world conflicts. We have our role to play in all of this.

J. Edsel Edmunds

The Triangle of Success can help you discover and develop your enormous potential and give expression to many new horizons. We are all born with inherited streams of abilities awaiting discovery.

Unfortunately, some of us become so fixed on a narrow path that we do not give full expression to our many endowed talents. Some of us discover them late in life, while others never at all.

Take the example of a spider separated from its parents. This young spider, without schooling or direction from its parents, can weave a complex web, sometimes several feet in diameter. This tells us that this creature has the innate ability to perform a seemingly difficult task without the tutelage of its particular society.

We too have enormous inherent potentials to achieve great things for and by ourselves and for humanity. The norms of our society and the influence of our human environment sometimes suppress the expression of our inherited abilities, but as we grow, we can gradually discover and give expression to our

The Triangle of Success

suppressed abilities, unlocking segments of our imprisoned inner selves.

Generally, we use only a rather small part of our brain. We need to expand our knowledge base by using more of our brainpower.

In this context, we must not suppress the dreams and aspirations of our youth, when those dreams relate to achieving high goals based on role models, and even what appear to be impossible dreams. Some children dream of being policemen, firemen, pilots, doctors, space travelers and various imaginary fields.

Dreams may manifest themselves in different forms at different times and stages of our human development and experience. Sometimes they remain fixed. For example, my wife always dreamt of being a teacher. She held on to that dream in spite of discouragement from her mother who tried to impress upon her that there was no money in teaching. Today, she enjoys the profession of teaching and the feeling of contributing to the development of young students. Her sister dreamt of being a lawyer, and after many years of practice as a qualified nurse, she began to study law. She is now a practicing lawyer who is assisting and helping young students defend their rights in the school system.

We must remember that there are many people in need, therefore think beyond selfish motives and reach out to help others. In this regard, a little help can go a long way in saving a life or giving inspiration to those who feel dejected. A little food to eat, something to drink, a kind word of encouragement to the young can save lives and improve humanity.

A young man, who was about to commit suicide by jumping from a high bridge, heard the words "we love you" and in a split second he changed his mind about jumping. He had never heard those words before. He broke down in tears and embraced the person who spoke the words. Today, he lives in a new world of discovered love and shares it with his fellow men.

Our triangle of success should include the goal to reach out to help others in need with the self-confidence that can make a difference, if we embrace a conscious plan to be of service to our communities. If we develop this personal attribute, our world could become a better place in which to live as a result of our outreach beyond self.

FOLLOWERS/LEADERS

> IN EVERY HUMAN BEING THERE IS THE PROPENSITY TO PLAY A LEADERSHIP ROLE WITHIN A LEADERSHIP SYSTEM

FOLLOWERS/LEADERS

Volumes have been written on the subject of leadership. Much less has been written on the specific subject of followers as leaders within the fabric of our societies and the success that could emanate there from.

"He/she was a born leader" is a phrase often ascribed to great leaders. The fact is that we all start out as followers in our early stages of life and gradually develop to be leaders or play leadership roles later in life.

Initially, babies convincingly express themselves to take care of their physiological needs which are provided by their parents or guardians. Later in life, as they develop, they follow by example and sometimes are made to act under strict rules imposed upon them by family, those in their environment, or those in authority. Early influences impact on the future behavior of individuals.

In some, leadership qualities may be manifested early in their development, whereas, in others, this is manifested later in life. We often do not recognize the leadership roles in those who follow, for we are not always aware of group dynamics and the value of participation by individuals playing a role as leaders in interactive group activities.

A greater appreciation of the potential of youth within our societies, and a conscious effort to mobilize, motivate, and empower them to assume leadership roles within our communities, would contribute to their greater influence in bringing about change for the betterment of our world.

It must not be assumed that leadership qualities are only attributed to the visible "front line" decision-making person of an establishment, corporation, or governing body. Followers, or workers in those organizations can also be leaders within a leadership system as vital components in an integrated arena of successful accomplishments. If you examine the working of a clock, you will realize that it takes many components or parts to make it work. Human societies are comparable to a clock, where each part is important for the successful working of the system.

The Triangle of Success

The effective and efficient working of the system can only be achieved through coordinated actions, where the parts assume their role for the benefit or achievement of the objectives of the whole. So it is with the individuals, nations, and regions of the world. We should recognize the interdependence of the small and the large segments of human societies and the importance of interpersonal and interdependent relations for success.

Following from the above, one could infer that in every human being is the ability to play a leadership role within a leadership system, the parts being as important as the whole. With changes in the system, you may develop to be the one playing the dominant leadership role. For example, the floor cleaner in a large or small institution may lead by example and may be promoted to the rank of supervisor. The freshman student through his/her acquired learning, experience, motivation, and empowerment, may, with time, become a vibrant leader within his institution and eventually become its leader.

In every life situation, you have the propensity as followers to lead from within and effectively assert yourself in a system in many different ways.

The above is intimately related to *The Triangle of Success*, for no matter how small you may be as a cog in the machinery of life, you are an important element for the success of any endeavor upon which you embark. You must therefore believe in yourself, set your goals, and execute an action plan to achieve them for we are all followers and leaders within the human system of life.

THE DIAMETER OF KNOWLEDGE: THE AREA OF THE UNKNOWN

AS WE INCREASE THE DIAMETER
OF OUR KNOWLEDGE
WE SHOULD BECOME AWARE OF
THE AREAS OF OUR IGNORANCE
WHAT WE KNOW IS
INFINITESIMALLY SMALL
COMPARED TO WHAT WE DO
NOT KNOW

THE DIAMETER OF EXISTING KNOWLEDGE AND THE AREA OF THE UNKOWN

A circle, its diameter and area are presented as geometric dimensions, or measures to conceptualize, or represent existing knowledge versus what we do not know, i.e. our areas of ignorance.

If the diameter of a circle is made to represent our existing knowledge, and its area to represent what we do not know, it should become evident as illustrated in Table 1, that as we increase the diameter of our knowledge we automatically increase the area related to what we do not know.

It becomes evident that the ratio of the diameter to the area is exponential in character i.e. not in a simple linear relationship. Further, this relationship involving the ratio of unknown to known grows infinite as our knowledge increases, demonstrating the vast unknown which surrounds us.

J. Edsel Edmunds

If you wish to challenge your existing knowledge as compared to what you do not know, you may ask yourself a few questions such as, how much do you know about the trillions of celestial objects millions of miles away? How much do you know about the trillions of micro and macro organisms living above and below the ground and in our oceans, and the facts related to the many academic and technical fields which are taught in our institutions?

Unfortunately, present teachings in some of our institutions of higher learning have become so narrow and specialized that little attention is paid to the interrelatedness of one field of study with another and insufficient coverage is given to the humanities.

It is by expanding our knowledge base that we can develop a better appreciation of the world around us, understand the differences and commonalities of humankind and become more aware of the extent of our ignorance. The hypothesis conceptualizing the circle, and its area, as they relate to knowledge, point to the need for us to expand on the diameter of our knowledge, and at the same time, expose the magnitude of our ignorance.

The detailed technical treatment of this hypothesis is the subject of another publication but it is presented here to excite curious minds to ponder on the infinity of knowledge, for, the source of knowledge is infinite, so is knowledge itself.

This is all related to *The Triangle of Success* where, in our pursuit for knowledge, we should realize that possibilities for engagement in different avenues of learning and human enterprises are infinite. This should encourage us to delve into uncharted fields without fear, for we must become masters of our destiny through the expansion of our knowledge base.

In this context, belief-in-self and application of an action plan in achieving goals could bring further fulfillment and success to us and to others.

J. Edsel Edmunds

TABLE 1
THE RELATIONSHIP BETWEEN
DIAMETER AND AREA

DIAMETER	**AREA**	**MULTIPLE**
UNITS	SQUARE UNITS	**INCREASES** OVER UNIT 1
1	.79	
2	3.14	4
3	7.07	9
4	12.56	16
6	28.26	36
8	50.24	64
10	78.50	99

DEVELOP A HOBBY

EXPLORE AND UNLEASH YOUR ENORMOUS POTENTIAL BY DEVELOPING A HOBBY

DEVELOP A HOBBY

I strongly recommend that you develop a hobby as an avenue for the expression of your mind and creativity, beyond your confined trained interests.

The pursuit of a hobby helps in the development of the right and left sides of the brain. It is to be noted that most of us produce less than our capabilities. The left side of the brain is attributed to areas related to logic, analytical thinking, language, reasoning, mathematics, and sciences. On the other hand, the right side is attributed to imagination, intuition, creativity, and the arts (music, dancing and related fields).

We, therefore, have within us, enormous untapped potential which should be explored and unleashed. If we do, we will discover the greatness within us and give expression to the powers bestowed upon us by Our Creator.

In my case, although I am a scientist by training, I have developed an interest in poetry, and published a book of ninety-nine poems entitled "Many Horizons".

I have also absorbed myself in painting and now have over one hundred personal pieces which I display from time to time at various galleries. My creative mind enables me to combine different media where I use acrylic paints on canvas with aluminum foil, ice, mulch, cloth, ashes and to modify driftwood as a form of sculptured expression.

It is never too late to explore both sides of the brain. Some people become fully aware of their potential late in life and even after retirement. For example, I know of doctors who have developed their artistic skills after giving up their practice while others of the same profession who have become building contractors and expert mechanics, while still practicing their profession.

Pause for a while and think about persons you know who have excelled in fields other than their field of training. These examples may represent the mobilization of the potential embedded in both sides of the brain.

The Triangle of Success

There are many areas we can think of beyond the confines of our particular training. I, therefore, exhort you to open up both sides of your brain to the fullest potential of your being. Learn another language, do creative things and discover your inner potential. You have it all within you, but you must unlock the doors and give expression to the other side of you which lies dormant and awaits exploration.

I have taken up the writing of poetry and painting as my hobbies, in spite of my scientific training and I am finding that there is no conflict in my various endeavors. In fact, my scientific schooling has been an asset to my artistic creativity. As a scientific researcher who studied Nematology, (the study of microscopic worms which attack plants) I do not feel constrained in my artistic creations. For example, I have developed "Yard Art" as an outdoor expression of an art form, whereas the majority of people confine art to the inner space of their homes. In my residential area of several thousand persons, the front and back of our home is the only residence displaying "Yard Art". It is a joy to observe our neighbors walk by in admiration of my creations.

J. Edsel Edmunds

I use the concept of *The Triangle of Success* to achieve success in my various goals in life while I continue to expand my knowledge base as much as I can. You may wish to do the same.

SELECTED RELATED PRESENTATIONS BY AUTHOR

1. Edmunds, J.E., Strive to achieve the highest Plateau of Success. Oakwood College Student Body. Huntsville, Alabama. October 15, 1986.

2. Edmunds, J.E., Think beyond the Peripheries of your Existing Knowledge. Commencement Exercise at the University of the Virgin Islands. St. Croix Campus. May 5, 1991.

3. Edmunds, J.E., Hard Work, Pursuit of Excellence and Discipline. Commencement Exercise at St. Mary's College, Castries, St. Lucia, West Indies. July 4, 1991.

4. Edmunds, J.E., The Community College, Meeting the Challenges of Today and Tomorrow. Commencement Exercise at Sir Arthur Lewis Community College,

St. Lucia, West Indies. December 8, 1991.

5. Edmunds, J.E., Global Humanism in Public Policy and International Affairs. Graduation Ceremony, Graduate School of Public Policy and International Affairs. University of Pittsburgh. April 26, 1997.

6. Edmunds, J.E., Human Capital and National Development. Commencement Exercise at the University of St. Martin. Philipsburg, St. Maarten, Netherlands Antilles. May 26, 2001.

7. Edmunds, J.E. Global Humanism, Man's Moral Responsibility. Panel Presentation on "Global Responsibility in the 21st Century, Group/Corporate and National Responsibility." Howard University, January 31, 2003.

ABOUT THE AUTHOR

The author, Dr. Joseph Edsel Edmunds, was the Ambassador of St. Lucia to the United Nations (1984-1989), the Organization of American States, and the United States of America (1984-1997), and a former Senator in the Government of St. Lucia. He is a graduate of the University of Puerto Rico (BSA in Agronomy) and Cornell University (MSc. and Ph.D in Plant Pathology and Nematology, respectively), and has been a researcher at the University of the West Indies. He served in an advisory capacity to countries in the South Pacific, Africa, Latin America, and the Caribbean in areas of his expertise.

He has also authored a book of ninety-nine poems entitled "Many Horizons." Additional, his poems have been published in books and Caribbean Anthologies. As an artist, his paintings have been exhibited in galleries and institutions in North America and the Caribbean.

Dr. Edmunds has received many prestigious awards, including the Order of the British

Empire, the Martin Luther King Legacy Award, and The Bernardo O'Higgins Grand Cross Award. The nematode *Longidorus edmunsi* was named in his honour for his outstanding contribution to the field of Nematology.

In a CITATION of 2000 by the St. Lucia National Trust, he was recognized as a pioneer in the conservation movement of St. Lucia and a Founding Member of the Trust. He has also been recognized by the Caribbean Council for Science and Technology as an Icon in Science, Technology and Innovation.

In the course of his activities as a scientist, statesman, diplomat, artist and poet, he has been addressing youth groups and institutions in the Caribbean and North America with the purpose of motivating and empowering them to achieve their potential.

This book is an embodiment of his presentations over many years and an expansion of his booklet on the same subject published in 2003.

Your outstanding achievements as a scientist, statesman, diplomat, artist, poet and international consultant serve to underscore the essence of your message in *The Triangle of Success*. Your presentation to the AlphaMax Academy was uplifting, empowering and inspiring. One of my students exclaimed "What Dr. Edmunds said was so clear that, if that is what it really takes, I am ready to take on the world and be a real success – no matter what."

Sean Taylor
Principal and Director
AlphaMax Academy
Suriname

The Triangle of Success will stimulate students – middle-school through early college and young people generally – towards the achievement of success in every aspect of lifelong learning and accomplishments. The book is concisely and simply written in a student-friendly fashion, which can be indelibly imprinted on students' minds for recall and guidance.

Melvin E. Jenkins
Professor Emeritus
Howard University
Washington, DC

As a member of a family of six, a parent of three and a teacher for over ten years, I wish I had been exposed to The Triangle of Success many years ago. I would have been more successful in my personal pursuits and in my contribution to family, students and the world. This book should become compulsory reading for students, parents, teachers and youth groups. I recommend it to you.

Barbara Best
Teacher
D.C. Public School, Choice Academy High School
Washington, DC

Printed in the United States
91755LV00003B/1-90/A